Acknowledgement of Land & of the Traditional Owners of this Land

I would like to acknowledge the Gadigal people of the Eora Nation, upon whose stolen land I stand on today.
I recognise that this land was never terra nullius — the land belonging to these peoples was never ceded, given up, bought or sold.
I would like to pay my respects to Aboriginal Elders past, present and emerging, and I extend this acknowledgement to all Aboriginal and Torres Strait Islander people.

In the year 2525

"In the year 2525, if man is still alive
If woman can survive, they may find...

In the year 3535
Ain't gonna need to tell the truth, tell no lie
Everything you think, do and say
Is in the pill you took today.

In the year 4545
You ain't gonna need your teeth, won't need your eyes
You won't find a thing to chew
Nobody's gonna look at you.

In the year 5555
Your arms hangin' limp at your sides
Your legs got nothin' to do
Some machine's doin' that for you.

In the year 6565
You won't need no husband, won't need no wife
You'll pick your son, pick your daughter too
From the bottom of a long glass tube.

In the year 7510
If God's a coming, He oughta make it by then
Maybe He'll look around Himself and say
Guess it's time for the judgment day.

In the year 8510
God is gonna shake His mighty head
He'll either say I'm pleased where man has been
Or tear it down, and start again.

In the year 9595
I'm kinda wonderin' if man is gonna be alive
He's taken everything this old earth can give
And he ain't put back nothing.

Now it's been ten thousand years
Man has cried a billion tears
For what, he never knew, now man's reign is through
But through eternal night, the twinkling of starlight
So very far away, maybe it's only yesterday.

In the year 2525, if man is still alive
If woman can survive, they may find...

Songwriters: Richard Lee Evans
Performed by: Zager & Evans

"I live in an Asylum"
"It is called…"
"…SOCIETY!"

CONTENTS

1: Control Your Emotions
(*Controlla le tue Emozioni*)
2: Have Fun!
(*Divertiti!*)
3: All in Good Time
(*Tutto in Tempo Utile*)
4: Mind Fuck
(*Mente Scopare*)
5: Just Put it Out into the World
(*Basta Metterlo Fuori nel Mondo*)
6: See Uniqueness in **Everyone**
(*Vedere l'unicità in tutti*)
7: I LO♥E this Weather
(*Amo questo Tempo*)
8: We All Have Garbage to Carry
(*Abbiamo Tutti Spazzatura*)
9: The Seeker
(*Colui che Cerca*)
10: When Hell Breaks Loose
(*Quando l'Inferno Frena Allentato*)
11: Don't Play with Me (Cause You Play with Fire)
(*Non Giocare con Me (perché giochi con il fuoco)*)
12: Age Disgracefully
(*Invecchiare Vergognosamente*)
13: You Can't Let Others Dictate What You Want to Do
(*Non Puoi Lasciare che Siano gli Altri a Dettare ciò che vuoi Fare*)
14: You Have Become a Machine
(*Sei Diventato una Macchina*)
15: Dirty Cock
(*Cazzo Sporco*)
16: Dangerous Ideas
(*Idee Pericolose*)
17: Success
(*Successo*)
18: Bad Girl for LO♥E
(*Cattiva Ragazza per Amore*)

CONTENTS

19: I Am Not Afraid of Dying
(Non ho Paura di Morire)
20: The Sound of Silence
(Il Suono del Silenzio)
21: A New Life, A New Society, A New World
(Una Nuova Vita, Una Nuova Società, Un Nuovo Mondo)
22: Don't Be a Prick!
(Non essere uno Stronzo!)
23: We Are NOT the Centre of the Universe
(Non Siamo il Centro dell'Universo)
24: Watching the Earth Burn
(Guardare la Terra Bruciare)
25: Wired
(Cablato)
26: Into The Valley of Death
(Nella Valle della Morte)
27: Anything Can Happen
(Tutto può Succedere)
28: There Are No Rules
(Non ci sono Regole)
29: Traumatised
(Traumatizzato)
30: Lies
(Bugie)
31: Fears
(Paure)
32: Active Non-Violence
(Non Violenza Attiva)
33: Create Your Own Reality
(Crea la tua Realtà)
34: Gravity
(Gravità)
35: Keep On Rockin'
(Continua a Rockin')

CONTENTS

36: Boulevard of Broken Dreams
(Viale dei Sogni Infranti)
37: The Cabala
(La Cabala)
38: Open Your Eyes
(Apri gli Occhi)
39: If I Could Grow a Garden
(Se Potessi Coltivare un Giardino)
40: (You're) Under Pressure
((Sei) Sotto Pressione)
41: We are Not Made of Plastic (So let's Drink Beer)
(Non Siamo Fatti di Plastica (Quindi Beviamo Birra))
42: The Apocalypse
(L'apocalisse)
43: Too Old
(Troppo vecchio)
44: Don't Follow Like Sheep!
(Non Seguire Come Pecore!)
45: (I'm Going) Insane
((Sto Diventando) Pazzo)
46: This Moment (is precious)
(Questo Momento (è Prezioso))
47: Living in an Asylum
(Vivere in un Asilo)
48: I Got the Blues
(Ho il Blues)
49: Stand Up!
(In Piedi)
50: (The Writings of a) Brain-Dead
(Scritti di un) Cervello Morto)

Control Your Emotions
(Controlla le tue Emozioni)

Do not let them take over.
Do not let them dictate terms.
Do not let them direct your actions.
Do not let them control you.
You must learn to...
... control your emotions.

Don't be ruled by your HE♥RT.
I'm not saying not to have a HE♥RT.
I'm saying, let it be a balance between *HEAD & HE♥RT*.
An equilibrium.
That is why...
...you must learn to...
... control your emotions.

Emotions will use anything to support their actions.
They will soon have you believing in...
... the supernatural.
... mysticism.
...spirituality.
... weird-arsed rituals (such as incantations, spells, mantras etc)
... praying to God.
... worshipping the Devil.
... looking for leprechauns at the bottom of the garden.
Pretty soon you'll be believing that "pigs can fly".
There's a man in the moon
& it's made out of cheese.
That is why...
...you must learn to...
... control your emotions.

"The Don"
13.10.2021

Have Fun!

(Divertiti!)

Don't take life seriously.
Life is too short.
You only have one life.
Don't waste it.
So...
...have fun!

Enjoy your life.
Be *curious*.
Be *interesting*.
Be *interested*.
Be *creative*.
Be *positive*.
Be *optimistic*.
Have fun!

Don't be *boring*.
Don't be a *Zombie*.
Don't be *morose*.
Don't be *negative*.
Don't be a *"doomsayer"*.
Don't be a *winger*.
Have fun!

"The Don"
09.11.2021

All in Good Time

(Tutto in Tempo Utile)

No point *rushing*.
No point *pushing*.
No point *hurrying*.
No point *forcing*.
No point *demanding*.
Everything will happen...
...*all in good time.*

Be *patient*.
Be *cool*.
Be *respectful*.
Be *kind*.
Be *generous*.
Be *caring*.
Everything will work out.
All in good time.

Don't *force*.
Don't *manipulate*.
Don't *strategise*.
Don't *fake it*.
Don't *embellish*.
Don't *theorise*.
Don't *Hypothesise*.

Everything will work out.
All in good time.

Be *optimistic*.
Be *positive*.
Everything will work out.
All in good time.

"The Don"
10.11.2021

Mind Fuck

(Mente Scopare)

Have you ever heard of a *"Mind Fuck"*?
Have you ever experienced one?
It's mental fucking.
There is no physical contact whatsoever.
It's all in the mind.
This is a "Mind Fuck".

No touching is involved.
There is no penetration.
Everything is mental.
It's all in the mind.
This is a "Mind Fuck".

It's not for everyone.
But then, it's not meant to be.
It's only for those that like to use their minds.
Because...
...it's all in the mind.
This is a "Mind Fuck".

Are you up for a *"Mind Fuck"*?
Do you think your mind can handle it?
It'll blow your mind.
This is what it's supposed to do!
Because...
...it's all in the mind.
This is a "Mind Fuck".

"It's all about energy transfer"

"Try a "Mind Fuck" today."
"You won't be disappointed!"
"And there is no mess to clean up afterwards."

"The Don"
10.11.2021

Just Put it Out into the World

(Basta Metterlo Fuori nel Mondo)

Just put it out into the world.
And walk away.
You've done your job.
Your work here is done
It's no longer your responsibility.
And let the world take it up.
Let the World do what it will with it.
Just put it out into the world.
And let the world do the rest.

Open your *space*.
Open your doors.
Open your *guts*.
Open your *feelings*.
Open your *fears*.
Open your *desires*.
Open *yourself*.
Just put it out into the world.
And let the world do the rest.

Exchange your *ideas*.
Exchange your *heart*.
Exchange your *soul*.
Exchange your *imagination*.
Exchange your *mind*.
Just put it out into the world.
Just let it all out.
And let the world do the rest.

Just put it out into the world.
And let the world do the rest.

"The Don" & Miriam
10.11.2021

See Uniqueness in Everyone

(Vedere l'unicità in tutti)

Everyone is different.
Everyone has their own individual personalities.
Their own particular peculiarities.
Their own identity.
Their own way of *seeing*.
...*feeling*
...*thinking*
...*loving*.
...*fearing*.
...*suffering*.
...*healing*.
Their own way of *happiness*.
See uniqueness in everyone.

Open your *eyes*.
Open your *mind*.
Open your *soul*.
But most importantly...
...open your HE♥RT.
And you shall see uniqueness in Everyone.

"The Don" & Miriam
10.11.2021

I LO♥E this Weather

(Amo questo Tempo)

I LO♥E the *sun*.
I LO♥E the *heat*.
I LO♥E the *rain*.
I LO♥E a *rainy day*.
I LO♥E the *wind*.
I LO♥E *storms*.
I LO♥E *lightning*.
I LO♥E *mist*.
I LO♥E *fog*.
I LO♥E this weather.

I hate the *sun*.
I hate the *heat*.
I hate the *rain*.
I hate *rainy days*.
I hate when it's *windy*.
I hate *storms*, they scare me.
I hate *lightning*, it's very frightening.
I hate *misty* days, they're too spooky.
I hate *foggy* days, you can't see a thing.
I LO♥E this weather.

"I must say, I LO♥E this weather!"
"Don't you just LO♥E this weather?"
"Nooooooooooooooooooo!"

"The Don"
12.11.2021

We All Have Garbage to Carry
(Abbiamo Tutti Spazzatura)

We all have burdens.
We all have a cross to carry
We all have a past weighing on our shoulders.
We all have garbage to carry.

We have no choice in the matter.
But it's what we do with this garbage.
It's how we deal with it that's important.
Because...
...we all have garbage to carry.

Do I let it fester & ferment?
Do I let it's stench envelope me?
Do I let its putrid smell proceed me?
Do I let it define me?
Do I let it control me?
Because...
...we all have garbage to carry.

"I don't want any dramas!"

"How do I smell this morning?'

"Can I help you with your load?"

"The Don"
12.11.2021

The Seeker

(Colui che Cerca)

Are you a *searcher?*
Are you a *wanderer?*
Are you an *enquirer?*
Are you a *questioner?*
Are you a seeker?

What do you seek?
...*money?*
...*fame?*
...*prestige?*
...*security?*
...*power?*
...*pleasure?*
...*happiness?*
... *LO*♥*E?*
...*immortality?*
...*enlightenment?*
...*the meaning of LIFE?*
Are you "The Seeker"?

Make sure you seek the right things.
Because...
...you might get what you seek for.

"The Don"
12.11.2021

When Hell Breaks Loose
(Quando l'Inferno Frena Allentato)

Hades has exploded.
Hell's Gate is open.
The *"Hellhounds"* have broken their chains.
The evil has been freed.
All the demons have escaped.
Blood is flowing in the *"River Styx"*.
The *"Ferryman"* is dead.
When Hell breaks loose.

Be scared.
Run & hide.
Close your mouth.
Shut your eyes.
Block your ears.
Cover your face.
Tremble in terror.
Protect your children.
When Hell breaks loose.

The Earth is on fire.
The land is parched.
The sky is red.
The Sun is the colour of blood.
The air is toxic.
The water is undrinkable.
The fish are committing suicide.
Birds are falling down from the sky.
When Hell breaks loose.

The zombies are stalking the streets.
Society is disintegrating.
Law & order has broken down.
There is looting in the streets.
The streets are on fire.
The drains are filled with blood.
Humans have become heartless.
Humanity has disappeared.
When Hell breaks loose.

Where will you be?
Where will you go?
What will you do?
When Hell has come to Earth.
When Hell breaks loose.

Whom will you spend your last days with?
When Hell breaks loose.

"Like hello, it's already broken loose!"
"Hellmouth is open!"

"The Don"
14.11.2021

Don't Play with Me (Cause You Play with Fire)
(Non Giocare con Me (perché giochi con il fuoco))

I'm on *fire*.
I am *hot*.
I'll *fuck* you.
I'll *play* with you.
I'll *burn* you.
So...
... don't play with me (cause you play with fire).

If you touch me...
... you'll get your fingers burnt.
If you hold me...
... your arms will melt.
If you kiss me...
...your lips will fuse together.
If you fuck me...
...your cock will incinerate.
So...
... don't play with me (cause you play with fire).

Don't even think about playing with me.
Cause you'll get burnt.
So...
... don't play with me (cause you play with fire).

So...
... don't play with me (cause you play with fire).

"The Don"
15.11.2021

Age Disgracefully

(Invecchiare Vergognosamente)

Take drugs...
...smoke dope.
...drop *ACID*.
...snort *Cocaine*.
...take *"Ecstasy"*.
Rage like there's no tomorrow.
Party like it's 1999.
Go CRAAAAZZZZZZZZYYYYYY.
Go WILD.
Because it's better to age disgracefully...
...than to age gracefully.

Don't *retire from life.*
Live until you drop.
Don't *conform.*
Don't *be comfortable.*
Be *uncomfortable.*
Be *adventurous.*
Take *risks.*
Age disgracefully.

Get *lowdown.*
Get *dirty*
Get *singing.*
Get *dancing.*
Make LO♥E.
Be *passionate.*
Be *"BAD".*
Be *"naughty".*
Be *creative.*
Age disgracefully

"Be like me!"
Age disgracefully.

"The Don"
15.11.2021

You Can't Let Others Dictate What You Want to Do
(Non Puoi Lasciare che Siano gli Altri a Dettare ciò che vuoi Fare)

Be your own boss.
Be in charge of your own life.
Take control of your future.
Take control of your destiny.
Don't let others take control.
Don't let others control you.
You can't let others dictate what you want to do.

Be who you want to be.
Do what you want to do.
See whomever you want to see.
Go where you want to go.
Fuck whomever you want to fuck.
LO♥E whomever you want to LO♥E.
Be whomever you want to be.
You can't let others dictate what you want to do.

Be free!
Be happy!
Don't let others dictate what you want to do.
Be yourself.
Without inhibitions.
Without limits.
Without boundaries.
You can't let others dictate what you want to do.

"The Don"
15.11.2021

You Have Become a Machine

(Sei Diventato una Macchina)

You can't feel.
You are a *hybrid*.
You are a *"Borg"*.
You are a *robot*.
You are an *"automaton"*.
You have become a machine.

You are no longer Human.
You have lost your Humanity.
You no longer have a HE♥RT.
You no longer have a Soul.
You no longer can LO♥E.
You no longer have a mind.
You have become a machine.

You now don't have a mind of your own.
You are now programmed.
You are governed by logarithms.
You are now controlled.
You cannot make decisions of your own.
You do not have a mind of your own.
You do whatever you are instructed.
You have become a machine.

"This does not compute!"

"This does not compute!"

"This does not compute!"

"This does not compute!"

"The Don"
15.11.2021

Dirty Cock

(Cazzo Sporco)

Why don't men share clothes?
Women share clothes.
Why?
Could it be something to do about the...
...dirty cock syndrome?

You play dirty.
You don't play by the rules.
You break the rules.
You make up your own rules.
You have the dirty cock syndrome.

You are a user
You are a taker.
You never give.
You don't like to share.
You always put yourself first.
That's the dirty cock syndrome.
Do you suffer from the dirty cock syndrome?

"The Don"
15.11.2021

Dangerous Ideas

(Idee Pericolose)

Seeing.
Hearing.
Feeling.
Doing.
Caring.
Respecting.
These are Dangerous Ideas.

Questioning.
Thinking.
Disagreeing.
Speaking out.
Protesting.
Campaigning.
Opposing the Government.
Rebellion.
Revolution.
These are Dangerous Ideas.

Do not harbour such ideas.
Do not contemplate such ideas.
Do not enact such ideas.
Do not promote such ideas.
Do not organise such ideas.
Do not carry out such ideas.
These are Dangerous Ideas.

Think for yourself.
Question everything.
Rebel when you disagree.
Start a revolution when you want change.
These are Dangerous Ideas.

Dangerous Ideas are too HOT to handle.
For the System.
For the Establishment.
"Do not entertain these Dangerous Ideas."

"The Don"
15.11.2021

Success

(Successo)

So, you see yourself as successful.
You have a great paying job as a banker.
You have a beautiful trophy wife.
You have 2 perfect children...
...a boy & a girl.
You wear designer clothes from Emilo Zen.
You have a Rolex on your wrist...
...you wear moccasins on your feet...
... with white socks & white yachting shorts....
...a loose fitting, cream linen shirt.
You have a great big house....
...in a gated community.
...in the exclusive part of town.
You only eat organic food.
Your drink of choice is Dom Perignon champagne.
You drive a Porsche SVU.
You like to snort a line or two of cocaine every day.
You have a beautiful life.
You live a 5 star life in a 1 star world.
You are a success story.

But...
...are you a success in what really matters?
...are you a success in happiness?

"Tell me, can success buy you happiness?"

"The Don"
15.11.2021

Bad Girl for LO♥E

(Cattiva Ragazza per Amore)

She's dangerous.
She's a pleasure machine.
She seeks pleasure with whomever she likes.
Wherever she likes.
She takes no prisoners.
She's a bad girl...
...a bad girl for LO♥E.

Don't fall for her charms.
Of which she has many.
Don't play her games.
You won't win.
She knows all the tricks.
She cannot be defeated.
Because...
...she's a bad girl...
...a bad girl for LO♥E.

Don't get snared in her web.
Don't be lured by her scent.
Although it is intoxicating.
Don't be enchanted by her cute looks.
They are there to trap you.
Don't be taken by her child-like innocence.
She's just toying with you.
Just like a cat playing with a mouse...
...before she has it for dinner.
Don't fall for her charms.
Because...
...she's a bad girl...
...a bad girl for LO♥E.

Never fall in LO♥ with her.
You will be burnt.
Because...
...she's a bad girl...
...a bad girl for LO♥E.

"The Don"
16.11.2021

I Am Not Afraid of Dying
(Non ho Paura di Morire)

Dying does not scare me.
I do not fear dying.
Not anymore.
Because I know what I am.
I know who I am.
I know where I'm going.
That's why I am not afraid of dying.

I am made of *"Star stuff"*.
I come from the stars.
An that's where I'll be going.
Back from whence I came.
From the *"Cosmos"*.
That's why I am not afraid of dying.

I'm going back to *"La Luna"*...
...back with *"Il Sol'*.
...back to the *"cosmic gases.*
...back to the *"Celestial Energy"*.
...back to *"Mother"*.
... back to the *Universe.*
That's why I am not afraid of dying.

Back to my home.
Back to the Universe.

"The Don"
16.11.2021

The Sound of Silence

(Il Suono del Silenzio)

I tried to speak...
... but I could not.
I tried even harder...
…this time louder...
...still nothing.
I tried even harder...
...I tried shouting.
...but still nothing.
I was becoming concerned...
...so, I tried yelling...
.... however still nothing.
Now I was getting angry...
...this time I started screaming...
... NOTHING!

Not a single sound.
Only the sound of silence.

I had lost my voice.
Not a single sound.
Only the sound of silence.

Only the sound of silence.

Only the sound of silence.

Only the sound of silence.

Only the sound of silence.

"The Don"
16.11.2021

A New Life, A New Society, A New World

(Una Nuova Vita, Una Nuova Società, Un Nuovo Mondo)

We have to build a new life.
We have to build a new self.
We have to build a new me
We have to build a new human.
We have to build a new society.
We have to build a new Life, a new Society, a new World.

This life is fucked.
This self is fucked.
This me is fucked
This Human is fucked.
This society is fucked.
This world is fucked.
We have to build a new Life, a new Society, a new World.

A life without shit.
A self without shit.
A me without shit.
A Human without shit.
A society without shit.
A world without shit.
We have to build a new Life, a new Society, a new World.

This is the only answer.
This is the only way.
This is the only way to save ourselves.
This is the only way to be Human.
This is the only way for a new society.
This is the only way for a new world.
We have to build a new Life, a new Society, a new World.

A better life.
I better self.
A better me.
A better Human.
A better society.
A better world.
We have to build a new Life, a new Society, a new World.

A simpler life.
A simpler me.
A simpler self.
A simpler Human.
A simpler society.
A simpler world.
We have to build a new Life, a new Society, a new World.

We have to escape the...
...old life.
...old me.
....old self.
...old Human.
...old society.
...old world.
We have to build a new Life, a new Society, a new World.

This is the only way to save ourselves.
We have to do it ourselves.
We have to leave it behind.
Move to the country.
And start a-new.
Start a-fresh.
Start again.
Start from scratch.
Leave this old society & old world behind.
We have to build a new Life, a new Society, a new World.

This is the only way!

"The Don"
17.11.2021

Don't Be a Prick!

(Non essere uno Stronzo!)

I said the wrong thing.
I didn't think.
I said what I thought.
She got offended.
She got hurt.
She said...
..."Don't be a prick!"

I was taken aback.
I hadn't expected that.
I never thought that.
I didn't mean to hurt her.
I didn't mean to make her cry.
She said...
..."Don't be a prick!"

I quickly apologised.
I said I was sorry.
"I didn't intend it that way."
She wasn't satisfied.
She said...
..."Don't be a prick!"
Just…
..."Don't be a prick!"

"The Don"
17.11.2021

We Are NOT the Centre of the Universe
(Non Siamo il Centro dell'Universo)

We think that the Universe revolves around us.
We think that we are the centre.
We think that we are THAT important.
That everything revolves around us.
In fact, it's the exact opposite.
We are NOT the centre of the Universe.

Such *hubris*.
Such *arrogance*.
Such *contempt*.
Such *conceit*.
Such *blindness*.
Such *stupidity*.
Such *madness*.
We are NOT the centre of the Universe.

We are not even a speck in the *cosmic ocean*.
We are not even *cosmic gases*.
We are not even a blink in the *"eye of the cosmos"*.
We are not even a footnote in the *"Celestial History Book"*.
We are NOT the centre of the Universe.

We no more important than the bacteria in our gut.

We are NOT the centre of the Universe.

"The Don"
17.11.2021

Watching the Earth Burn

(Guardare la Terra Bruciare)

Our beds are burning.
Whilst we are sleeping.
Wake up!
Wake up!
Can't you see the smoke?
Aren't you chocking on its fumes?
Where there is smoke there is fire.
Don't just sleep...
... *while the Earth is burning.*

Don't stand still.
There is fire below your feet.
The Earth is burning.
Your feet are on fire.
You are on fire.
You are burning.
You're paralysed just...
... *watching the Earth burn.*

Shout out.
"Fire!"
"Fire!'
"The Earth's on fire."
Scream!
"Wake up!"
"Wake up!"
"The Earth is burning."
But no one is listening.
No one wants to hear.
We are all just sitting around...
...... *watching the Earth burn.*

We're just sitting...
...... *watching the Earth burn.*

"The Don"
18.11.2021

Wired

(Cablato)

I'm *tied up.*
I'm *ensnared.*
I'm *trapped.*
I'm *caught.*
I'm *strung up.*
I'm *strung out.*
I'm *caught in a net.*
I'm a *puppet.*
I'm a *pawn.*
I'm *not free.*
I'm wired.

I have no *choices.*
I have no *freedom.*
I have no *independent thoughts.*
I have no *imagination.*
I have no *feelings.*
I have no HE♥RT.
I have no *soul.*
I am wired.

I have no *past.*
I have no *future.*
I have no *present.*
I have no *LIFE.*
I have no *DEATH.*
I have *NOTHING.*
Because...
...*I am wired.*

"The Don"
18.11.2021

Into The Valley of Death

(Nella Valle della Morte)

Forwards we matched.
All in a line.
One after the other.
A slow monotonous shuffle.
Our feet barely getting off the ground.
It was as if we were in pray.
But in actual fact, we were comatose.
As we slowly marched…
…into the Valley of Death.

Marching from our past.
Marching from the present.
Marching to our future.
Marching to our doom.
Marching like lemmings to their slaughter.
Marching to our extinction.
Marching…
…into the Valley of Death.

The death tune was playing.
The death song was singing.
The death sounds echoed in the valley.
The death buzzards flew overhead.
The death clouds were shouting out a warning.
The death rain fell like blood.
The death enveloped us…
…as we matched…
…into the Valley of Death.

"The Don"
18.11.2021

Anything Can Happen
(Tutto può Succedere)

There are *infinite possibilities*.
There are *a myriad number of alternatives*.
There are *infinite consequences*.
There are *indefinite futures*.
That's why...
...*anything can happen*.

Every action has *a consequence*.
Every action has *energy*.
Every action has *power*.
Every action has *life*.
Every action has *death*.
So be careful what actions you carry out.
Because...
...*anything can happen*.

Be prepared for *all possibilities*.
Be prepared for the *unexpected*.
Be prepared for the *unforeseen*.
Be prepared for the *unforeseeable*.
Be prepared for anything.
Because...
...*anything can happen*.

Don't *fret*.
Don't *frown*.
Don't *sweat*.
Don't *panic*.
Don't *fear*.
Because...
...*anything can happen*.

The Universe acts without limits.
Be when the Universe acts...
...*anything can happen*.

"The Don"
18.11.2021

There Are No Rules

(Non ci sono Regole)

The lawmakers make the laws.
The police enforce them.
We blindly follow them.
The criminals break them.
The lawyers make money from them.
But...
...if you have money...
...*there are no rules.*

Only…
...*the poor.*
...*the meek.*
...*the sick.*
...*the feeble of mind.*
...*the fools.*
Follow the laws.
Because if you are powerful...
...*there are no rules.*

Those that make the laws *break them.*
The law enforcers *break them.*
The politicians *break them.*
The lawyers *break them.*
The rich *break them.*
The poor *break them.*
Everyone *breaks them.*
Because everyone knows that...
...*there are no rules.*

"The Don"
18.11.2021

Traumatised

(Traumatizzato)

I'm *paralysed*.
I'm *comatosed*.
I'm *confused*.
I'm *frightened*.
I'm *terrorised*.
I'm *hypnotised*.
I'm *entranced*.
I am traumatised.

I can't *see*.
I can't *hear*.
I can't *move*.
I can *feel*.
I can't *think*.
I can't *sleep*.
I can't *dream*.
I am traumatised.

I am *stuck*.
I am *immobilised*.
I am *stoned*.
I am *afraid*.
I am *feverish*.
I am *terrorised*.
I am *horrified*.
I am traumatised.

"The Don"
18.11.2021

Lies

(Bugie)

Everyone lies.
That is the truth.
That is the only truth.
Do not believe what is said.
Because...
... *everyone lies.*

Your parents *lie.*
Politicians *lie.*
Priests *lie.*
LO♥ERS *lie.*
You *lie.*
I *lie.*
Everyone lies.

It's all lies.
There is no *"pot of gold at the end of the rainbow."*
There is no *happy ending.*
There is no *truth.*
There is no *future.*
There is no *democracy.*
There is no *justice.*
There is no *fairness.*
It's all lies.

Do not believe *anything.*
Do not believe *anyone.*
Do not believe *politicians.*
Do not believe *religious leaders.*
Do not believe *your LO♥ERS.*
Do not believe *yourself.*
Everybody lies.

Everything is one big fat lie.
That is the ONLY truth.
Everything is a lie.
Everyone lies.

Don't Believe a thing!
It's ALL lies!

"The Don"
19.11.2021

Fears

(Paure)

What do you fear?
Do you fear...
...loneliness?
...rejection?
...abandonment?
...insecurity?
...sickness?
...childlessness?
...imagination-less?
...mindlessness?
...thoughtlessness?
...soul-lessness?
...emptiness?
...LO❤ELESSNESS?
...mortality?
...DEATH?
Maybe you fear all of these.

Whatever you fear, understand that...
...all your fears are illusory.

"The Don"
19.11.2021

Active Non-Violence

(Non Violenza Attiva)

Want to change *society*?
Want to bring down the *Establishment*?
Want to get rid of the *government*?
Want to build a *better world*?
Want to be a *rebel*?
Want to have a *revolution*?
Active Non-Violence is the way.
Active Non-Violence is the methodology.

Do not fight violence with violence.
That only creates more violence.
Fight violence with its opposite...
... *Active Non-Violence*.
It's like mixing an acid with an alkali.
It's a *"neutralisation reaction"*.
Acid + Alkali = salt + water.
Violence + Active Non-Violence = a new society.
Do not fight *fire* with *fire*.
Suffocate it.
Remove its Oxygen.
Fight violence with Active Non-Violence.

Mahatma Gandhi did it.
Martin Luther King did it.
Václav Havel did it
We can do it.
We create a vacuum for violence.
We neutralise violence.
We have the methodology.
We have the technology.
If there are enough of us.
We must be organised.
Active Non-Violence is the methodology.

Active Non-Violence is not just a methodology for social change.
Active Non-Violence is also a methodology for personal internal change.
We individually have to introduce *Active Non-Violence* into our own behaviour.
We individually have to live using *Active Non-Violence*.
In...
...*our behaviour*.
...*our thinking*.
It has to become part of our very being.
There should be no violent thoughts or actions.
Never!
Ever!
This is *Active Non-Violence*.
This is the only way.
For permanent positive changes.
The internal + the external.
Individual change + social change = permanent change.
This is Active Non-Violence.

"The Don"
20.11.2021

Create Your Own Reality

(Crea la tua Realtà)

Create your own *reality*.
Live you own *reality*.
Otherwise, you will be living someone else's *reality*.
Construct the *reality* you want to live in.
There are only 2 alternatives...
... either you create your own reality.
Or...
...you live in someone else's reality.
Wouldn't you rather live in a *reality* built by you?
Create your own reality.

A *reality* that suits your values, ideals & principles.
A *reality* that only has your peps.
A *reality* that you have built.
This is your *reality*.
This is your world.
This is your life.
It's the only way.
To...
...create your own reality.

Create your own *reality intentionally*.
Create your own *reality methodically*.
Create your own *reality purposefully*.

Reality is subjective!

"LO❤E your reality!"
"Live your own reality!"
Create your own reality.

"The Don"
20.11.2021

Gravity

(Gravità)

Gravity pulls us down.
Gravity has weight.
Gravity makes us heavy.
Gravity weighs on us.
Gravity holds us to the ground.
Gravity enchains us to the ground.
Gravity is dense.
Gravity is heavy.
Gravity is a burden.
Gravity is affects all of us.
Gravity cannot be escaped.
Gravity is everywhere.
Gravity is a force to be reckoned with.
Gravity is powerful.
Gravity is relentless.
Gravity never let's go.
Gravity never gives up.
Gravity affects my body.
Gravity affects my muscles.
Gravity affects my mind.
Gravity affects my thoughts.
Gravity affects my imagination.
Gravity affects my HE♥RT.
Gravity affects my soul.
Gravity cannot be escaped.
"Gravity, is serious!"

"The Don"
20.11.2021

Keep On Rockin'

(Continua a Rockin')

Never *stop rockin'*.
Never *lose the rockin'*.
Never *stop being a rebel*.
That's what rock & roll is all about.
So, keep on rockin'.

Make sure to rock on.
No matter the situation.
No matter who you're with.
No matter what's happening.
No matter if you're told not to.
Just keep on rockin'.

Keep on *rockin' in the morning*.
Keep on *rockin' at lunchtime*.
Keep on *rockin' in the afternoon*.
Keep on *rockin' into the evening*.
Keep on *rockin' in bed*.
Keep on *rockin' when you're sleeping*.
Just keep on rockin'.

Keep on rockin'!

Never stop rockin'.
Keep on *rockin' until you drop*.
And even then, *keep on rockin' even MORE!*

"Yeah, keep on rockin' girl!"

"The Don"
20.11.2021

Boulevard of Broken Dreams
(Viale dei Sogni Infranti)

That's where all your unfilled dreams go to die.
All those dreams you had but never saw the light of day.
All those dreams that were abandoned along the way.
All those dreams that you tried to achieve but failed at.
All those dreams from your innocent youth when anything seemed possible.
All those dreams from your idealistic rebellious years.
All those dreams from your adult years climbing the career ladder.
All those dreams that you abandoned as you entered old age.
All those dreams that you realised were "pie in the sky dreams".
All those dreams that were just unreachable.
All those dreams that were taken away from you by happenstance.
All those dreams that were taken away from you by a "simple twist of fate".
All those dreams that were taken from you by a cruel society.
All these dreams can be found in the Boulevard of Broken Dreams.

"The Don"
20.11.2021

The Cabala

(La Cabala)

The Chakras.
The flow of internal energy.
The map to *"Enlightenment"*.
The *"Cosmic Design"* inside all of us.
The flow of *"Universal Energy"*.
This is the Chakra.

Study it.
Understand it.
Practice it.
Implement it.
Use it.
Live by it.
Die by it.

The Cabala is your roadmap.
The Cabala is your pathway.
The Cabala is your journey.
The Cabala is your life.

"The Don"
21.11.2021

Open Your Eyes

(Apri gli Occhi)

Open your eyes.
Look around you.
Take a really good look.
What do you see?
Do you like what you see?
Are you happy with what you see?
Open your eyes.

Do you see the *destruction?*
Do you see the *cruelty?*
Do you see the *discrimination?*
Do you see the *hatred?*
Do you see the *violence?*
Do you see the *inhumanity?*
Do see the *wanton destruction of the environment?*
Open your eyes.

Open your eyes.
What do you see?
Open your eyes.
Look around you.
What do you see?
Do you like what you see?
Are you happy with what you see?
When you open your eyes.

"The Don"
20.11.2021

If I Could Grow a Garden

(Se Potessi Coltivare un Giardino)

*"If I could grow a garden.
With all the mistakes I see every day...
...the garden would be amazing!
Flowers would have the most incredible colours.
It would be populated with the most exotic plants from all over the world.
If I could grow a garden.
With all the mistakes I see every day."*

The Garden of Eden would just be unkept, overgrown weeds.
The Hanging Gardens of Babylon would no longer be hanging.
The Gardens of Versailles would be a wild, vast wilderness.
The Boboli Gardens would be just parched earth.
*If I could grow a garden.
With all the mistakes I see every day.*

*"If I could grow a garden.
With all the mistakes I see every day.
I would water the plants every day.
I would treat them like my best friends.
I would talk to them.
Tell would them how beautiful they are every day.
I would make LO♥E to them.
If I could grow a garden.
With all the mistakes I see every day."*

"This would be my garden."

"The Don" + Miriam
20.11.2021

We are Not Made of Plastic (So let's Drink Beer)
(Non Siamo Fatti di Plastica (Quindi Beviamo Birra))

If you can't handle it, drink milk.
Otherwise, drink beer.
There is something in the hops.
It opens up your *mind*.
It opens up your *attitude*.
It opens up *who you really are*.
"I LO♥E drinking beer!"
If you can't handle it, drink milk.
We are not made of plastic (so let's drink beer).

I smoke.
I drink beer.
I smoke pot.
I swear a lot.
I fart a lot too.
I offend everyone.
People just can't handle me.
If I offend you…
…you can just FUCK off.
We are not made of plastic (so let's drink beer).

I'm ok drinking my beer & smoking my pot.
In fact, *I FUCKING LO♥E it!*
FUCKING LO♥E it!
So, if you can't handle it, drink milk.
Otherwise, drink beer.
Lots of it!

We are not made of plastic (so let's drink beer).

"Anyway, just FUCK off!"

"The Don" + Miriam
20.11.2021

(You're) Under Pressure

((Sei) Sotto Pressione)

You're under the *pump*.
You're under the *thumb*.
You're *trampled underfoot*.
You're *submerged under water*.
You're *working for the man*.
You're *in the fire*
You're *in the shit*.
You're *all over the place*.
You're *carrying a heavy load*.
You're *out of control*.
You're *dissatisfied with your life*.
You're *not going to take it anymore*.
You're *going crazy*.
You're *a loser*.
You're *losing your religion*.
You're *going to lose your mind*.
You're *at your wits end*.
You're *going insane*.
You're *overthinking*.
You're *"blind as a bat"*.
You're *dazed & confused*.
You're *on fire*.
You're *a burning bush*.
You're *buying a "Stairway to Heaven"*.
You're *"Knocking on Heaven's door"*.
You're *facing your Future*.
You're *at the end of the road*.
You're *at the end of your time*.
You're *out of time*.
You're *at the end of the line*.
You're *a zombie*.
You're *one of the "Walking Dead"*.
You're *Dead*.
You're *NOTHING*.
You're UNDER PRESSURE.

"The Don"
21.11.2021

The Apocalypse

(L'apocalisse)

Are you ready?
Have you *prepared yourself?*
Have you *put your affairs in order?*
Have you *said your goodbyes?*
Have you *fulfilled your bucket list?*
Have you *realised your dreams?*
Have you *had a good life?*
Have you *been happy?*
Have you LO♥ED?
Have you been LO♥ED?
Have you been a *good person?*
Have you been a *decent person?*
Have you *tried to right wrongs?*
Have you *been kind?*
Have you *been caring?*
Have you been *compassionate?*
Have you tried to *end wars?*
Have you tried to *make this a better society?*
Have you tried to *make this a better world?*
Have you *got a clear conscience?*
Have you *slept well at night?*
Have you *made peace with yourself?*
Have you *made peace with others?*
Have you LO♥ED yourself?
Have you *prepared yourself?*
For the Apocalypse is COMING!

I have seen the "*Four Riders*" in the sky.
Whose names are…
…Pestilence.
…War.
…Famine.
…& Death.
For the Apocalypse is HERE!

"The Don"
22.11.2021

Too Old

(Troppo vecchio)

You're just too old.
Too old...
...to cuddle to.
Too old...
...to kiss.
Too old...
...to go to bed with.
Too old...
...to have sex with.
Too old...
...to fuck.
Too old...
...to see your cock.
And it's a very old cock by the way!
Too old...
...to make LO♥E to.
Too old...
...to have a relationship with.
Too old...
...to rock & roll.
Too old...
...to dance with.
Too old...
...to sing with.
You're just too old for me.
In fact, you're just TOO old!

You should just go off & die!
Because you're just TOO old!

You're just an old *"fart'!*
You're just TOO old!

"The Don"
22.11.2021

Don't Follow Like Sheep!
(Non Seguire Come Pecore!)

Don't be *led*.
Don't be *ushered*.
Don't be *herded*.
Don't be *fodder*.
Don't be *a servant*.
Don't be *a slave*.
Don't be *manipulated*
Don't be *harassed*.
Don't be *pushed*.
Don't be *shoved*.
Don't be blind.
Don't be *silenced*
Don't be *silent*.
Don't be *deaf*.
Don't be *dumb*.
Don't be *stupid*.
Don't be *victimised*.
Don't be *objectified*.
Don't be *abused*.
Don't be *violated*.
Don't be *subjectified*.
Don't be *sacrificed*.
Don't be *crucified*.
Don't be *slaughtered*.
Don't be *murdered*.
Don't be *killed*.
Don't be *meat*.
Don't just be a *bag of "blood & bones"*.
Don't be *mind-less*.
Don't be *a robot*.
Don't be *a machine*.
Don't be *dehumanised*.
Don't follow like sheep!

Don't *go in*.
Don't *give in*.
Don't *acquiesce*.
Don't *appease*.
Don't *accept*.
Don't *tolerate*.
Don't *excuse*.
Don't *lie*.
Don't *sleep*.
Don't follow like sheep!

"We are NOT sheep!"
"So, don't act like sheep!"
"Don't follow like sheep!"

"The Don"
22.11.2021

(I'm Going) Insane

((Sto Diventando) Pazzo)

This is not my *comfortable bed.*
This is not my *beautiful, exotic girlfriend.*
This is not my *beautiful, luxurious bedroom.*
This is not my *ruggedly handsome face.*
This is not my *beautifully sculptured body.*
This is not my *friendly, cuddly, pet dog.*
This is not my *nutritiously, organic breakfast.*
This is not my *stylish, handmade "Emilio Zen" jacket.*
This is not my *beautiful, exclusive 5 bedroom house.*
This is not my *beautiful red electric, convertible sports car.*
This is not my *fantastic, highly remunerated job.*
This is not my *fabulous, amazing career.*
This is not my *friendly & quaint English local pub.*
This is not my *favourite, thirst quenching beer.*
This is not my *wonderful best friend.*
This is not my *beautiful "soulmate".*
This is not my *beautiful harbour city.*
This is not my *beautiful, egalitarian country.*
This is not my *beautiful & protected natural environment.*
This is not *my caring society.*
This is not my *wonderful world.*
This is not my *beautiful, "Blue" planet.*
This is not my *wonderfully full & rewarding life.*
This is not my *beautiful future.*
This is not my *beautiful Death.*

This is my *worst, horrible nightmare!*
I must be going...
...*INSANE!*

I'm going INSANE!
I'm going INSANE!
I'm going INSANE!
I'm going INSANE!

"The Don"
23.11.2022

This Moment (is precious)

(Questo Momento (è Prezioso))

This Moment is *irreplaceable*.
This moment is *priceless*.
This moment is *unique*.
This moment is but a *"blink of an eye"*.
This moment is *transient*.
This moment is *impermanent*.
This moment is *temporary*.
This moment is *indefinable*.
This Moment is *precious*.
This moment is *glorious*.
This moment is *amazing*.
This moment is *"Gold"*.
This moment is so *easily lost*.
This moment cannot *be captured*.
This moment cannot *be stopped*.
This moment cannot *be frozen in time*.

Enjoy "This Moment"!
Before it is gone!
Before it's TOO late!

This Moment is precious.
This moment is there to be seized.
Don't miss the opportunity.
It won't come again.
Treasure it.
You are so lucky to be experiencing this.

"Seize this moment!"

"The Don"
23.11.2021

Living in an Asylum

(Vivere in un Asilo)

This is a madhouse.
The world has gone crazy.
There is madness on the streets.
The Earth's on fire.
Society is in disarray.
Politicians are liars.
Governments manipulate the population.
Corporations rule the world.
The media is setting the agenda.
Making up any shit they want.
Rupert Murdoch is laughing all the way to the bank.
To deposit another billion or twenty.
The Earth is getting hotter every second.
But Government's don't give a shit.
Fish have had enough.
They're committing suicide by the hundreds of thousands.
The youth are getting restless.
They know what it's all about.
They are the only ones that care.
Is anybody listening to them though?
No FUCKING way!
Nobody seems to care.
Nobody gives a flying FUCK!
They just sick back in their lounge chairs.
Hypnotised on Netflix.
Binging on the latest series.
What's it this time?
"Doomsday-The End of the world!"
Hahahahahahahah!
Watching the World being destroyed on TV.
This is the world that we live in, in 2021.
We're living in an asylum.
And there is no way out.
There is no escape.
EVER!

"But don't worry!"
"Don't panic!"
"It's ok!"
"We're living in an asylum."

"The Don"
23.11.2021

I Got the Blues

(Ho il Blues)

I got the Blues baby.
I got the Blues so bad tonight.
Because the gal I LO♥E is out with another man.
She met him on Tinder.
She met up with him other night.
She told me she kissed him.
But did not have sex.
So, I've got the Blues "real" bad.

Is she seeing him tonight?
Is she spending the night with him tonight?
Is she kissing him tonight.?
Is she fucking him tonight?
I'm all alone tonight.
All by myself listening to the Blues.
Because I've got the Blues tonight.

There's no point crying.
There's no point being sad.
There's no point being forlorn.
There's no point having a heavy heart.
She told me that I'm just too old for her.
She likes younger men.
So, that's why...
...I've got the Blues.

"The Don"
23.11.2021

Stand Up!

(In Piedi)

Stand up for *your rights*.
Stand up for *what you believe in*.
Stand up for *yourself*.
Stand up for *others*.
Stand up for the *weak*.
Stand up for the *poor*.
Stand up for the *disadvantaged*.
Stand up for the *abused*.
Stand up for the *exploited*.
Stand up for the *discriminated*.
Stand for *injustice*.
Stand up for *freedom*.
Stand for the *natural environment*.
Stand up for the *Amazon*.
Stand up for *Mother Earth*.
Stand up for *human rights*.
Stand up for *humanity*.
Stand up for *the future*.
Stand up!

You gotta stand up.
Just stand up & make yourself seen.
Stand up & make yourself be heard.
Just stand up!
You gotta stand up.
Stand up!

"The Don"
23.11.2021

(The Writings of a) Brain-Dead

(Scritti di un) Cervello Morto)

Don't *see!*
Don't *observe!*
Don't *read!*
Don't *write!*
Don't *discuss!*
Don't *converse!*
Don't *exchange!*
Don't *interact!*
Don't *communicate!*
Don't *theorise!*
Don't *hypothesise!*
Because you are "Brain-Dead"!

Don't *feel!*
Don't *act!*
Don't *react!*
Don't *move!*
Don't *object!*
Don't *reject!*
Don't *protest!*
Don't *disagree!*
Don't *contradict!*
Don't *rebel!*
Don't *LO❤E!*
Don't *THINK!*
Because you are "Brain-Dead"!

You are "Brain-Dead!"
"These are the writing of a Brain-Dead!"

"The Don"
05.08.2020

Books written by "The Don"

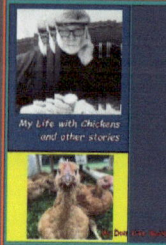

"My Life with Chickens & other stories: I Pity the Poor Immigrant"
*Published:
10th September, 2019
Autobiography Book 1:
0 – 12 years old*

"Poems for Misfits, Miscreants, Misanthropes, Mavericks, Losers & Malcontents!"
*Published:
10th June, 2020
Book of Poems 1*

"Poems for Troubled Minds & Trouble Hearts"
*Published:
10th August, 2020
Book of Poems 2*

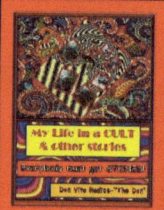

"My Life in a CULT & other stories: Everybody Must Get STONED!"
*Published:
10th September, 2020
Autobiography Book 2:
15 – 30 years old*

"Poems for Restless Minds & Restless Hearts"
*Published:
10th October, 2020
Book of Poems 3*

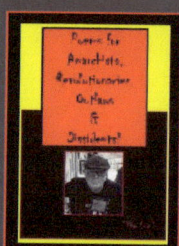

"Poems for Anarchists, Revolutionaries, Outlaws & Dissidents!"
*Published:
10th November, 2020
Book of Poems 4*

"Poems for Non-Thinkers & Eccentrics"
*Published:
10th December, 2020
Book of Poems 5*

"The Rantings of a Madman"
*Published:
10th January, 2021
Book of Poems 6*

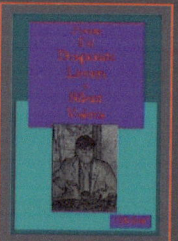

"Poems for Desperate Lovers & Silent Voices"
*Published:
10th February, 2021
Book of Poems 7*

"Poems for Tormented Minds & Tortured Souls"
*Published:
10th March, 2021
Book of Poems 8*

All available ONLY online

Books written by "The Don"

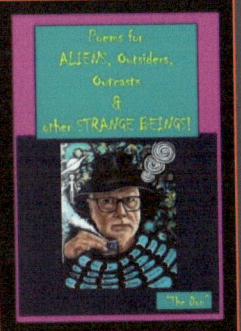

"Poems for ALIENS, Outsiders, Outcasts & other STRANGE BEINGS!"
Published: 10th April, 2021
Book of Poems 9

"Poems for Beings From Another Planet"
Published: 10th May, 2021
Book of Poems 10

"Poems for Mindless Beings & Lost Souls"
Published: 10th June, 2021
Book of Poems 11

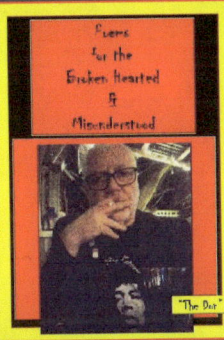

"Poems for the Broken Hearted & Misunderstood
Published: 10th July, 2021
Book of Poems 12

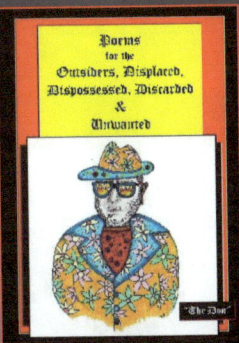

"Poems for Poems for the Bewildered, Dazed & Confused"
10th August, 2021

Book of Poems 13

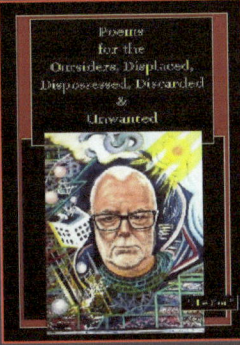

"Poems for the Outsiders, Displaced, Dispossessed, Discarded & Unwanted"
Published: 10th Sept, 2021

Book of Poems 14

All available ONLY online

"Poems for Secret Agents, Phantom Agents, Agents of Change, Agent Provocateurs & Agents of Chaos"
Published: 10th Oct, 2021
Book of Poems 15

"Poems for Disenchanted, Disillusioned & Delusional
Published: 10th November, 2021
Book of Poems 16

Books written by "The Don"

"Poems for the Stoners, drugos, ACID takers & Psychedelic LO♥ERS (Everybody Must Get Stoned)"
Published: 10th December, 2021
Book of Poems 17

"Poems for Anarchists, Rebels & Revolutionaries
Published: 10th January, 2022
Book of Poems 18

"Poems for Rebels, Radicals & Revolutionaries
(Viva la Révolution!)
Published: 10th February, 2022
Book of Poems 19

"Poems for Trouble Makers, Freaks
&
Lost Souls
Published: 10th March 2022
Book of Poems 20

**Vito Radice
("The Don")**
(Poet/Author/Polemicist/Non-Thinker/Non-Intellectual)
Email: vitoradice@gmail.com
Instagram: don_vito_radice
Facebook: Vito Radice
Mobile: +61490012461 (Australia)

www.ingramcontent.com/pod-product-compliance
Lightning Source LLC
Chambersburg PA
CBHW042048290426
44109CB00006B/154